This advice showing how to become
a perfect lady was originally
published in London in the 1890s.

"Those who have refined manners should pity those that are without."

THE LADY'S BOOK OF MANNERS

SHOWING
HOW TO BECOME A PEFECT LADY:
ALSO CONTAINING
LOVE, COURTSHIP, AND MARRIAGE

HOW TO TALK CORRECTLY;
POLITE AND ACCURATE
CONVERSATION
AND PRONUNCIATION;
COMMON ERRORS CORRECTED;

HOW TO READ;

AND A GUIDE TO THE ART OF
COMPOSITION AND PUNCTUATION.

Copper Beech Publishing

Published in Great Britain by
Copper Beech Publishing Ltd
This edition © Copper Beech Publishing Ltd 2006
Edited by Julie Hird and Jan Barnes

ISBN
1-898617-41-4
978-898617-41-9

A CIP catalogue record for this book is available from
The British Library.

Copper Beech Gift Books
Copper Beech Publishing Ltd
PO Box 159 East Grinstead
Sussex England RH19 4FS

Politeness in life

is ever more commanding than vulgarity.

Preface

The aim of this volume is to present the general
rules of politeness and etiquette in such a manner
as to render them plain and instructive, and be
indeed what it assumes as its title, a Book of
Manners, showing how to become a Perfect Lady.

The aim in every part of the book has been
to make a useful guide to the dining room,
the parlour, and other places where ladies
may properly be ambitious to appear
with satisfaction and honour to themselves,
and pleasure to others.

HOW TO BECOME A PERFECT LADY

Good manners are never out of fashion …

Politeness itself is always the same. A sincere regard for the rights of others in the smallest things (as well as in the largest) genuine kindness of heart; good taste, and self-command, which are the foundation of good manners, are never out of fashion. A person who possesses them can hardly be rude or discourteous.

Words and actions

Politeness seems to be a certain care, by the manner of our words and actions, to make others pleased with us and themselves.

The grand secret is to have an intention of always doing right.

Happiness

Trivial as these rules may appear to the unreflecting, nearly all the happiness which derives from society depends upon them.

Let no lady be afraid of learning life's courtesies; they contribute not only to her own but other peoples' comfort.

PERSONAL HABITS

Make your own person the first lesson

Personal habits must be specially regarded, and placed in proper order and refinement.

No right to offend others

Attention to the person is the first necessity of good manners. Therefore make your own person the first lesson. The proper care and adornment of the person is a social as well as an individual duty. You have a right to go about with unwashed hands and face, and to wear soiled garments, perhaps, but you have no right to offend the sense of others by displaying such hands, face, and garments in society.

Those who have refined manners
should pity those that are without

CLEANLINESS

Not necessarily vulgar

Keep yourself scrupulously clean, not just your hands and face, but your whole person, from the crown of your head to the soles of your feet.

Dirty feet

Silk stockings may hide dirty feet, but ankles often reveal themselves when the lady little dreams of such an exposure. It is far better to dress coarsely and out of fashion and be *strictly* clean, than to cover a dirty skin with the finest clothing. A coarse calico dress is not necessarily vulgar, but dirt is essentially so.

Soiled hands

Soiled hands are an honour in the field, but in a country in which soap and water abound there is no excuse for carrying them into the parlour or the dining room.

You should wash the whole body with pure soft water
every morning on rising from your bed,
rubbing it till dry with a coarse towel,
and afterwards using friction with the hands.

THE DAILY BATH

Use good, fine soap

To keep clean you must bathe frequently. Wash the whole body with pure soft water every morning on rising from your bed, rubbing it till dry with a coarse towel, and afterwards using friction with the hands.

Cold bathing

If you have not been at all accustomed to cold bathing, commence with tepid water, lowering the temperature by degrees till that which is perfectly cold becomes agreeable. In warm weather comfort and cleanliness alike require still more bathing.

But the daily bath is not sufficient. In addition to the pores (from which exudes the fluid called perspiration), the skin is furnished with innumerable minute openings, known as the sebaceous follicles. Also, especially in warm weather, they emit a *very* disagreeable odour.

A thorough rinsing

Pure cold water will not wholly remove these oily accumulations. The occasional use of soap and warm or tepid water is therefore necessary; but all washings with soapy or warm water should be followed by a thorough rinsing with cold water. Use good, fine soap. The common coarser kinds are generally too strong alkaline, and have an unpleasant effect upon the skin.

THE FEET

Frequent washings

The feet can become offensive in smell, especially when the perspiration is profuse. Frequent washings with cold water, with the occasional use of warm water and soap, are absolutely necessary to cleanliness. *Such ablutions have a tendency to cure and prevent corns.*

THE NAILS

If you allow the nails to get too long

A lady will not go into company, or sit down to the table, with soiled hands and nails. Clean them carefully every time you wash your hands, and keep them smoothly and evenly cut. If you allow the nails to get too long they are liable to be broken off, and become uneven, and if you pare them too closely they fail to protect the ends of the fingers.

CHANGE OF LINEN

Well aired every morning

A frequent change of linen is another essential of cleanliness. It avails little to wash the body if we enclose it the next minute in soiled garments.

It is not in the power of every one to wear fine and elegant clothes, but we can all afford to have clean shirts, drawers, and stockings. Never sleep in any garment worn during the day and your night-dress should be well aired every morning.

THE TEETH

❧

A lady will preserve her teeth till old age

Do not forget the teeth. Cleanliness, health, and a pure breath, require that they be thoroughly scoured with the tooth-brush dipped in soft water, with the addition of a little soap, if necessary, every morning.

Hasten to preserve

If your teeth have been neglected, and some of them are already decayed, hasten to preserve the remainder. While you have any teeth left, it is never too late to begin to take care of them.

Rules for a lady's teeth

Brush them outside and in, in every
possible direction.
After brushing, rinse your mouth
with cold water.
A slighter brushing should be given them
after each meal.
Use a tooth-pick or a quill to remove any particles
of food that may be lodged between the teeth.
By these simple means a lady will preserve her teeth,
in all their usefulness and beauty, till old age.

THE HEAD

Hair thoroughly brushed

The head is more neglected than any part of the body. Dandruff forms, dust accumulates and hair grows dry!

If the hair is thoroughly brushed
Washing will not injure the hair, but will promote its growth and add to its beauty. If soap is used, it should be carefully rinsed off. If the hair is *thoroughly* brushed every morning, it will not require frequent washings. If the scalp be kept in a healthy condition the hair will be glossy and luxuriant.

Night-caps are most unwholesome contrivances, and
should be discarded altogether. They keep the head
unnaturally warm and shut out fresh air. Ladies may
keep their hair properly together during repose
by wearing a net over it.

Night-caps are most unwholesome

Many ladies suffer for want of proper exercise. Ladies, if you would be healthy, beautiful, and attractive – if you would fit yourselves to be good wives, and the mothers of strong and noble children, you must *take a large amount of exercise in the open air. This should be an every-day duty.*

EXERCISE

Four or five hours per day spent in the open air

No person can enjoy vigorous health without a considerable degree of active bodily exertion. Four or five hours per day spent in the open air, in some labour or amusement which calls for the exercise of the muscles of the body, is probably no more than a proper average.

Those whose occupations are sedentary should seek amusements which require exertions of the physical powers, and should spend as much as possible of their leisure time in the open air.

Use good judgement

We must, however, use good judgement in this matter as well as in eating. Too much exercise at once, or that which is fitful and violent, is often injurious to those whose occupations have accustomed them to little physical exertion of any kind.

ON INTRODUCTIONS

Mutually agreeable and proper

The custom, which prevails in country places of introducing everybody you meet to each other, is both an annoying and an improper one.

As a general rule, introductions ought not to be made, except where there is undoubted evidence that the acquaintance would be mutually agreeable and proper. An introduction is a social endorsement, and you become to a certain extent responsible for the person whom you introduce.

Avoid the company

Should you have cause to avoid the company of any one to whom you have been properly introduced, be respectful towards him, while at the same time you may shun his society.

A lady's rules for proper introductions

Present the youngest person to the oldest.

Present the humblest to the highest in position.

The gentleman is always presented to the lady.

No gentleman should be presented to a lady
without her permission being previously obtained.

When you introduce parties which you are quite
sure will be pleased with each other, it is well to
add, after the introduction, that you take great
pleasure in making them acquainted.

Be careful to pronounce each name distinctly.

A lady's rules for proper introductions

When you are introduced to a person, be careful not to appear as though you had never heard of him before. Such an oversight would be unpardonable.

In introducing members of your own family you should always mention the name. Say, "My father Mr. Jones."

Ladies on being introduced, bow the head gracefully.

On a second meeting between two ladies the hand may be extended, but do not proffer your hand to a gentleman, unless you are very intimate.

LETTERS OF INTRODUCTION, &c.

An unpardonable recklessness

Letters of introduction are to be regarded as certificates of respectability. To send a person of whom you know nothing into the confidence and family of a friend is an unpardonable recklessness.

Call, or send a note, as early as possible
When a gentleman or lady with a letter of introduction to you, leaves his or her card, you should call, or send a note, as early as possible. There is no greater insult than to treat a letter of introduction with indifference.

Do not give a letter of introduction to anyone with whom you are not much acquainted. Enquire searchingly into his or her real claims on your regard, and do not hastily comply with his or her request.

Never address a letter of introduction to one of whom you have but a partial knowledge. Some people write in a friendly strain to one of whom they know but little more than the name.

Note paper of the best quality

Letters of introduction should be written on note paper of the best quality, and must be delivered unsealed to the party whom they are to introduce. The letter must be enclosed in an envelope. Never give such a letter unless you have a good opinion of the bearer. Permit your friend to fasten the envelope before you forward the letter to its destination, by which you give permission to read its contents.

STREET SALUTATIONS

Virtue of courtesy

Nowhere has a woman occasion more frequently to exercise the virtue of courtesy than on the street; and in no place is the distinction between the polite and the vulgar more marked.

If a lady addresses an inquiry to a gentleman on the street, he will lift his hat, or at least touch it respectfully, as he replies.

Neatly and in good taste

With regard to your dress in the street, you should dress neatly and in good taste and in materials adapted to the season. The full costume suitable to the carriage or the drawing-room is entirely out of place in a shopping excursion, and does not indicate a refined taste, it looks *snobbish*.

'When tripping over the pavement, a lady should gracefully raise her dress a little above her ankle. With her right hand she should hold together the folds of her dress and draw them towards the right side. To raise the dress on both sides, and with both hands is vulgar. This ungraceful practise can be tolerated only for a moment, when the mud is very deep.'

Loosely and gracefully

The out-door costume of ladies is not complete without a shawl or a mantle. Shawls are difficult to wear gracefully; a lady should not drag a shawl tight to her shoulders and stick out her elbows, but fold it loosely and gracefully.

At night time

In the night it would not be prudent for a young lady to walk alone. Should she be passing an evening with a friend, she should previously appoint some one to conduct her home at an appointed hour or she should politely ask the person visited to allow a servant to accompany her. Should the gentleman of the house offer to become your conductor, politely regret that you give him so much trouble; but modestly accept his guardianship. After arriving at your home, gratefully acknowledge your obligations.

A lady's rules for street salutations

It is a great rudeness not to return to a salutation, no matter how humble the person who salutes you.

Loud talking in the street is a sure sign
of ill breeding.

Never address a lady or gentleman on the opposite
side of the street, as to cause you to speak loudly.
This would be deemed very rude. It will be better
to give a gentle bow in case of recognition.

A married lady usually leans upon the arm of her
husband. Single ladies do not in the day time take
the arm of a gentleman, unless they wish to
acknowledge their engagement.

SHOPPING

❧

If the price seems to you too big

Having enjoined the most patient courtesy on the part of the shopkeeper, every civility ought to be reciprocal. Never say, *"I want such a thing,"* but, *"Show me, if you please, that article"*. If they do not show you at first the article you desire, and you are obliged to examine a great number, apologise for the trouble you give.

If you make small purchases, say, *"I am sorry for having troubled you for so trifling a thing."*

If you spend a considerable time in the selection of articles, apologise to the shopkeeper who waits for you to decide.

Do not trespass too much on the valuable time of the shopkeeper by your fastidiousness.

*If the price seems to you too big, and the shop has not
fixed prices, ask for an abatement in brief and civil terms,
and without ever appearing to suspect the good faith for
the shopkeeper. If he does not yield, do not enter into a
contest with him, but go away, after telling him politely
that you think you can obtain the article cheaper elsewhere,
but if not, that you will give him the preference.*

MORNING CALLS

Allow time for the lady's dinner toilette

Morning calls are very important and necessary, in order to maintain good feeling they must be carefully regarded. A morning call should be made between two and four p.m. in winter, and two and five p.m. in summer. Be sure to avoid luncheon hours when you pay a morning visit, and allow time for the lady's dinner toilette.

Even if politely requested

Half an hour amply suffices for a visit of ceremony. A lady may remove her boa or the silk handkerchief that enwraps the neck, but, on no account, either the shawl or bonnet, even if politely requested to do so by the mistress of the house. *Some trouble is necessarily required in replacing them, and this ought to be avoided.*

A lady's rules for making morning calls

Ladies should always be the first to rise in
terminating a visit, and when they have made their
adieux, their cavaliers follow them out.

Soiled overshoes or wet garments should not be
worn into any room devoted to the use of ladies.

Do not seem to notice any silent hint, by rising
hastily; but take leave with quiet politeness.

If, during your short visit, the conversation becomes
uninteresting, it will be best to retire.

When other visitors are announced, retire as soon as
possible, and yet without letting it appear that their
arrival is the cause.

A lady's rules when out in the morning

Young married ladies *may not* appear in a public place unattended by their husbands or elder ladies. This rule must not be infringed, in visiting exhibitions, public libraries, or promenades; but a young married lady may walk with her friends, married or single.

Shop windows, in large towns have attractions; but it is not desirable to be seen standing before them alone.

Be careful never to look back, nor to observe too narrowly the dresses of such ladies as may pass you.

Should any one address you seem not to hear, but hasten your steps.

A lady's rules when visiting a friend's house

If invited to spend a few days at a friend's house, conform as much as possible to the habits of the family. Inquire, when parting for the night, respecting the breakfast hour, and ascertain at what time the family meet for prayers. Give as little trouble as possible; and never think of apologising for the extra trouble which your visit occasions. *Such an apology implies that your friend cannot conveniently entertain you.*

Visiting cards should be engraved or handsomely written. Those printed from type are considered vulgar, simply, no doubt because they are cheap. A lady's card may be larger and finer, and should be carried in a card-case.

A lady's rules when receiving morning calls
In the country it is customary to offer refreshment
to morning visitors, but in town this is
not expected.

When morning visitors are announced, rise and
meet them. Invite the lady to the sofa; but if an
aged lady or gentleman, offer them an easy chair
and place yourself near them. Always pay due
respect to age and rank, and give them the most
comfortable seats; in winter near the fire.

When your visitors rise to depart, you must rise also,
and remain standing till they have left the room.
Call or ring for the servant to meet them in the hall,
and let them out.

DINNER PARTIES

Keep your eyes open and your wits about you

A young lady, unaccustomed to the observances of such occasions, can hardly pass through a severer ordeal than a formal dinner! Its terrors, however, are often greatly magnified. A knowledge of the points of table etiquette, complete self-possession, habits of observation and a fair share of practical good sense, will carry one safely through.

You may decline invitations to dinner parties without any breach of good manners, yet you are liable, at a hotel, or on board a steamer, to be placed in a position in which ignorance of dinner etiquette will be mortifying and the information contained here be worth a hundred times the cost of the book!

Keep your eyes open and your wits about you, *wait and see what others do,* and follow the prevailing mood.

A lady's rules for the routine of a fashionable dinner
Invitations should be sent seven days previous, or
other engagements could prevent some from
accepting.

It is a great breach of etiquette not to answer an
invitation as soon as it is received, and it is an insult
to disappoint when we have promised.

Letters or cards of invitation should always name
the hour of dinner.

Well-bred people will arrive as nearly at the
specified time as they can. Never allow yourself to
be a minute behind the time, and you should not
get there long before, unless the invitation requests
you come early for a little chat before dinner.

A lady's rules for dress at a fashionable dinner

Always go to a dinner as neatly dressed as possible.
The expensiveness of your apparel is not of much
importance, but its freshness and cleanliness are
indispensable.

A lady's 'full dress' is not easily defined, and fashion
allows her greater scope for the exercise of her taste
in the selection of materials, of colours, and style.

The dress of ladies should be simple, and according
to their bearing. Ladies ought to consider their
figure, and their stature.

The hands and nails require especial attention. It is
an insult to all at the table for persons to sit down to
dinner with their hands in a bad condition.

A lady's rules for arriving at a fashionable dinner

The dinner cannot be served till all the guests have arrived. If it is spoiled through your tardiness, you are responsible not only to your interests, but to all the guests. Better be late for the steamer or the railway train than for a dinner!

If a guest be late, or a cook unpunctual, the lady of the house must not appear displeased, but try to divert the minds of her guests with pleasant and agreeable conversation.

Ladies should reflect upon these remarks, and be modest and retired, not only in dress but in everything else.

It is awkward for both parties where visitors arrive before the lady of the house is ready for them. If it is necessary for the lady of the house to keep an eye upon the dinner, it is still best that she should familiarly receive her guests; and beg to be excused, if it is necessary for her to vanish occasionally to the kitchen. A real lady is not ashamed to have it known that she goes into the kitchen; on the contrary, it is more likely that she will be a little proud of being thought capable of superintending the preparing of the feast.

Arranging the guests

When dinner is on the table, the lady and gentleman of the house will have an opportunity of showing their tact by seeing that the most distinguished guests, or the *oldest*, are shown into the dining-room first. The lady should advance to receive her guests; the chairs should be arranged so as not to create any confusion on their entrance; and her welcome should be smiling and cordial.

Separate husbands from wives

It is one of the most difficult things properly to arrange the guests, and to place them in such a manner that the conversation may always be general during the entertainment. If the number of gentlemen is nearly equal to that of the ladies, take care to intermingle them. Separate husbands from their wives, because being always together they ought not to converse among themselves in a general party.

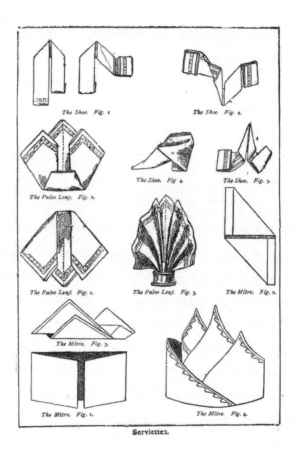

The Shoe. Fig. 1.

The Shoe. Fig. 2.

The Palm Leaf. Fig. 2.

The Shoe. Fig 4.

The Shoe. Fig. 3.

The Palm Leaf. Fig. 1.

The Palm Leaf. Fig. 3.

The Mitre. Fig. 2.

The Mitre. Fig. 3.

The Mitre. Fig. 1.

The Mitre. Fig. 4.

Serviettes.

MANNERS AT THE TABLE

The body should be kept in a tolerably upright position

Nothing more plainly shows the well-bred lady than manners at the table. They may be well-dressed, may converse well, but their manners at the table will be sure to expose them.

To be avoided

Any unpleasant peculiarity, abruptness, or coarseness of manners, is especially offensive at table. All such acts as leaning over on one side in your own chair, placing your elbows on the table or on the back of your neighbour's chair, gaping, twisting about restlessly in your seat, are to be avoided.

Deportment

Though the body at table should always be kept in a tolerably upright position, one need not sit bolt-upright, as stiff and prim as a poker. To be natural, and to appear comfortable, is the deportment required. Pleasant and lady-like habits at table are easily acquired, if you are careful to observe them at your own table daily.

Attain a polished ease

You will never attain a polished ease in society unless you practise its habits continually. You cannot *put on* a habit, or a graceful manner, when you will; it *must* be a thing of daily life. Care bestowed upon it will relieve you from the oppression of awkwardness and shyness in society.

Good manners as the hostess

Do not insist upon your guests partaking of particular dishes; never ask persons more than once, and never put anything by force upon their plates.

It is extremely ill-bred, though extremely common, to press one to eat of anything.

Most important

The most important maxim in hospitality is to leave everyone to his own choice and enjoyment, and to free him *from an ever-present sense of being entertained.*

Wait

You should never send away your own plate until all your guests have finished.

Signal

After dessert the hostess will give the signal to the ladies for retiring, by rising from the table.

Good manners as a guest

The soup

Soup will come first. *You will not decline it;* because to sit with nothing before you would be awkward. You may eat as little of it as you choose. You must not suck soup into your mouth or send for a second plate. In serving out soup, one ladleful is the utmost to be given.

Fish

The fish course is to be eaten with a fork aided by a piece of bread without vegetables. *(This part does not apply to informal dinners where fish is the principal dish.)* When you have eaten sufficient, lay your fork on your plate, and the waiter will remove it.

Principal dishes

The third course brings the principal dishes – roast and boiled meats and fowl, which are followed by game. There are also side dishes of various kinds.

Drink your soup as quietly as possible, from the side of the spoon. You, of course, will not commit the vulgarity of blowing in it, or trying to cool it, after it is in your mouth, by drawing in an unusual quantity of air, for by so doing you would be sure to annoy, if you did not turn the stomach of the lady or gentleman next to you.

Dessert

When the dessert comes on, finger glasses, filled with warm water, are brought round to the guests, in which, after wetting a corner of your napkin and wiping your mouth with it, you rinse your fingers.

At dessert, a gentleman will help the ladies near them to whatsoever they may require. Serve strawberries with a spoon, but pass cherries, grapes, or peaches for each to help himself with his fingers. They need not volunteer to pare an apple or a peach for a lady, but should do so, of course, at your request, using a fork to hold it.

The reason why it is considered impolite to take soup or fish a second time at a large party, is because by so doing you keep the rest of the company staring at you. It is the selfish greediness of this act, therefore, that constitutes its vulgarity.

A lady's guide to good manners at the table

It is looked upon as the height of vulgarity to use your knife to convey your food to your mouth.

Making a noise in chewing your food will get you a bad name at table among people of good breeding.

Avoid too slow or too rapid eating; the one will appear as though you did not like your dinner, and the other as though you were afraid you would not get enough.

Speak to a waiter in the tone of *request* and not of *command* or you will create, among well-bred people, the suspicion that you were sometime a servant yourself, and are putting on airs!

A girl with neatly and properly dressed feet, with neat, well-fitting gloves, smoothly arranged hair, and a clean, well-made dress, who walks well, and speaks well, and, above all, acts politely and kindly, is a lady, and no wealth is required here.

DRESS

Simple and elegant

Dress is often greatly modified by circumstances of time, place and condition. The beauty of dress consists in not being conspicuous. Dress ought to be simple and elegant, without being too expensive for the wearer. Ridiculous fashions *should never be adopted*. Everyone ought to dress with reference to her position in society.

First impressions

First impressions are generally most permanent, it is desired that they should be favourable ones. Be careful, therefore, to dress well, remembering that mental qualities are often judged by the exterior. A sensible and refined gentlewoman will never attire herself in a manner unbecoming either to her circumstances or her person.

In bad taste

A worsted dress on a warm day, or a white one on a cold day or a light thin one on a windy day are all in bad taste.

Very fine or very delicate dresses worn in the street, or very highly ornamented clothes worn to church, are in bad taste. Very long dresses worn in muddy or dusty weather, even if long dresses are the fashion, are still in *bad* taste.

Deep and bright-coloured gloves are always in bad taste; very few persons are careful enough in selecting gloves.

Light shoes and dark dresses, white stockings and dark dresses, dark stockings and light dresses, are all in bad taste.

Deportment

The secret of dress is deportment. Many ladies seem to imagine that because they are attired well they must necessarily pass current as such. What a mistake! Rude behaviour, or ill and awkward manners appear still more odious when coupled with an assumed gentility of dress.

Satin and lace

By dressing well, we do not mean dressing extravagantly. You might have the most costly attire, you might appear in satin and lace, feather, and jewels, and yet be far from being well dressed.

Harmonise with the colour

To wear pink and green, red and yellow together is very bad taste indeed. If the dress be of a full bright colour, as violet or a deep rich blue, the shawl of mantle should be black and the bonnet should suit and harmonise with the colour.

A slovenly appearance

Ladies should never wear an ill-fitting dress. It destroys the *contour* of the most perfect figure, and gives a slovenly appearance to an otherwise unexceptionable costume. Let the dress either fit to the shape, or be sufficiently loose to form graceful and natural folds.

A lady of advanced years

No lady will be the first to make her appearance in any new and peculiar style of dress: nor will a lady of advanced years assume the wardrobe of youth. Every age has its appropriate costume; what can be more out of character, than to see a face already shaded by the hand of time, decked out in ringlets. Never let an elderly lady use gaudy colours, or too many ornaments.

Tastefully arranged

Many ladies consider rather what is fashionable than becoming. Our short sisters persist in wearing a pyramid

of flounces, and even frills. Those who are advanced in years often forget that for every age a certain costume is advisable, necks should adorn a slight frill, or a tastefully arranged silk handkerchief.

Dress may heighten beauty, but it cannot create it.

Remember, the most important points are:

Well made shoes

Clean gloves

A nice pocket handkerchief

A graceful deportment

All of these are indispensable to a lady-like appearance.

CONVERSATION

Cultivate language and the voice

Conversation is a great and valuable accomplishment in society. Cultivate language and the voice. Learn to express yourself with correctness, ease, and elegance.

No one need despair

The natural qualities essential to the good talker are a clear, active intellect, warm human sympathies, frankness of disposition, and fluency of speech. Some ladies are therefore naturally better talkers than others and, though all may not hope to reach the highest excellence in conversation, no one need despair of being able to talk well.

Do not pretend to be what you are not, for no pretension can hide what you really are.

Being improved or developed

The faculty of language is susceptible of being improved or developed to an astonishing extent; and here, as in every other department of our nature, the means to be used is *exercise*.

Ease, confidence and self-possession are essential to your success as a conversationalist. If you are bashful and diffident, and consequently embarrassed and awkward in company, the difficulty must be met and overcome.

If you set yourself down as a 'nobody', society will be very likely to take you at your word.

Naturally excitable

Self-possession may be lost through excitement as well as through bashfulness, in which case you will be very apt to say things which you will afterwards regret. Guard against this fault, especially if you are naturally excitable.

Chaotic existence

Our ideas as well as our words should be so arranged that the connection between them shall clearly appear. We cannot reasonably expect to express clearly and effectively ideas which have only a chaotic existence in our minds.

Careless and slatternly

You may have the richest stores of information, inexhaustible funds of anecdote, the best habits of thought, and the most brilliant wit, and yet fail in conversation, through ignorance of the fundamental rules of the language you speak, or a careless and slatternly use of it.

Few can travel extensively, even in these days of steamship and railways, but books are accessible to all. Read, then, as much and as carefully as you can on all subjects of general interest, with a view to store up and use in conversation the information you may acquire.

A lady's guide to talking well

Warm affections are as necessary to the talker as a clear intellect. Only the words which come *from* the heart go *to* the heart.

To *talk* well, one must *think* well. Strict mental discipline and habits of consecutive thinking add greatly to the interest and value of a person's conversation.

Strive, then, to acquire methodical habits of thought. This will improve both your mind and your conversational powers.

Cultivate self-respect and self-reliance. Rich and varied stores of knowledge drawn from books, conversation, and observation, are invaluable.

A lady's guide to talking well

Master a subject completely if you can; but the
merest *smattering* is better than no information at all.

Carefully avoid talking either of your own or other
people's domestic concerns.

Talking of yourself is an impertinence to the
company; your affairs are nothing to them.

Giving advice, unasked, is another piece of rudeness.
It is, in effect, declaring ourselves wiser than those
to whom we give it.

You should never help out the slow speaker.

Do not talk too loud in company.

A matter of dispute

Those who contradict others and make every assertion a matter of dispute, betray, by this behaviour, a want of acquaintance with good breeding.

Trite sayings

Vulgarism in language is the distinguishing characteristic of a bad education. Proverbial expressions and trite sayings are the flowers of the rhetoric of a vulgar person.

Flattery

Never descend to flattery; but deserved compliments should never be withheld. If a lady's style of dress or manner of wearing her hair pleases you, you may certainly say so in proper terms, without giving offence.

Avoid these subjects

Controverted questions in politics, religion and social ethics should generally be avoided in mixed companies.

Harmless jokes

Whatever passes in parties at your own or another's house is never repeated by well-bred people. Things of no moment, and which are meant only as harmless jokes, are liable to produce unpleasant consequences if repeated.

A lady will remember

A real lady will avoid showing her learning and accomplishments in the presence of ignorant and vulgar people, who can, by no possibility, understand or appreciate them. It is presumptious for you to take it for granted that everybody present is anxious to listen to you, and you may, besides, disturb the conversation already going on between others. You will also avoid talking to any one across the room.

Avoid the use of slang terms and phrases in polite company.

Boasting

There is no surer sign of vulgarity than perpetual boasting of the fine things you have at home. If you speak of your silver, your jewellery, your costly apparel, it will be taken for a sign that you are either lying, or that you were, not long ago, somebody's washerwoman, and cannot forget to be reminding everybody that you are not so now.

A city woman

There is a type of city woman, who never gets into the country but they employ their time in trying to astonish the country people with narrations of the fine things they left behind them in the city. If they have a dirty little closet, with ten valueless books in it, they will call it their *library*. If they have some small room, that is used as a kitchen, parlour, and dining-room, they will magnify it into a *drawing room*.

About an absent friend

If you are in a company which violently abuses an absent friend of yours, you need not take up the club for her. You will do better by saying mildly that they must have been misinformed. After this, *if they are real ladies,* they will stop.

A fishmonger's style

Never address a person by his or her initial letter, as "Mr. C.," or "Mrs. S." It is as vulgar as a fishmonger's style.

ADDITIONAL REMARKS ON CONVERSATION

... the instant she opens her mouth ...

A woman is sure to show her good or bad breeding the instant she opens her mouth to talk in company. If she is a *real lady* she starts no subject of conversation that can possibly be displeasing to any person present. Everyone has been invited to be *agreeable* and to *please*.

Be a good listener

A sure way to please in conversation is to hunt up as many of each others' excellencies as possible, and be as blind as possible to each others imperfections. Listen attentively and patiently to what is said. It is a great and difficult talent to be a good listener, but it is one which the well-bred lady has to acquire.

Time your remarks, and make them fit.
Pleasantries of all kinds need timing.

Don'ts for ladies!

Don't appear dogmatic in any assertions you make.

Don't interrupt a person who is telling a story, even though she is making historical mistakes in dates and facts. It is not your business to mortify her by attempting to correct her blunders!

Don't use sarcasm in social parties. They are weapons which few can use.

Avoid exaggerated forms of speech. Never say *splendid* for pretty, *magnificent* for handsome, *horrible* for unpleasant, *immense* for large.

Don't insult a company by maintaining a contemptuous silence. Even if you are not a good talker, try to sustain some share of the conversation.

Don'ts for ladies!

Do not talk too much, do not *try* to talk, but whenever you speak, do so with self possession, and *always* look at the person you are addressing.

Avoid unnecessary excitement or enthusiam. Do not quench your ardour, but merely do not expose it to the world. For one time when we are liable to distress another by our acts and deeds, there are fifty, a hundred, or perhaps more, occasions when we are liable to do so by our words.

Avoid pomposity; be as correct and elegant in the use of language as you can, but do not ransack the dictionary for long and learned words. Common words for common things, is the rule.

To sum up, the qualities necessary for a good
conversationalist are:

a proper gravity,

an ease and fluency of expression,

a love of candour and truth,

a considerable tact,

a forbearance towards others,

an agreeable voice,

a gentleness of manner.

Story-telling in company is an art which few possess
in perfection. Story-telling is subject to two defects,
frequent repetition and being soon exhausted.

POSITION AND MOTION

Never be ashamed …

It seems a simple and easy thing to walk, to stand or sit, but not one in twenty performs these acts with ease and grace.

Out of place

When seated, a lady ought neither to cross her legs nor take any vulgar attitude. A lady should occupy her chair entirely, and not appear restless. It is altogether out of place for her to throw her drapery around her in sitting down, or to spread out her dress for display. In walking, a lady ought to have a modest and measured gait. A lady should not turn her head or stare about her; such a habit seems an invitation to the impertinent.

Never be ashamed to acquire the
smallest grace by study and practise.

IN THE DRAWING ROOM

Who has not rejoiced ..?

Delightful is the change from a heated dinner-room to the apartment appropriated for receiving company. Who has not rejoiced in such a transition? The freeness of the air, the beauty of the flowers which fashion assigns in a drawing room, the ready instruments of music, and the elegantly-bound books laid out for inspection: all awaken pleasant thoughts.

Introductions

Suppose you have not dined with the family; that it is an evening party you are invited to attend, then, when you enter, the lady will introduce you to the remainder of the ladies.

There is nothing more unsocial and unfriendly than non-introduction. Sometimes people who are really anxious to be introduced to each other remain perfect strangers in consequence of the non-observance of this very necessary custom.

Verbal invitations are highly disrespectful; it appears as though you thought they could be had at any time for the asking. It is best to be observant of small matters of politeness, even to our friends.

EVENING PARTIES

Do not allow bad weather to prevent your attendance

Evening parties are of various kinds and their object is social enjoyment.

Keep your promise

Having accepted an invitation to a party, never fail to keep your promise, and especially do not allow bad weather to prevent your attendance. Invitations to evening parties are sent several days before the party date. Answers should be returned immediately.

Nine o'clock is the hour which custom has established as the time for the lady to be in her parlour, ready to receive her guests, and by ten o'clock all the guests should arrive.

Rules for lady guests

Married ladies are usually attended by their husbands; but this is not absolutely necessary.

Unmarried ladies cannot go alone (if their mothers do not accompany them, they may go under the guardianship of a married sister).

When you enter the drawing room, look for the lady of the house, and speak to her before your friends. In leaving a party, before it breaks up, seek the lady of the house, and bid her good-night as quietly as possible.

Really well-bred ladies are *never* guilty of the sin of backbiting.

These unkind thoughts keep in your mind
and let them not expression find!

EVENING PARTIES – AMUSEMENTS

Music banishes the dark clouds of life

What would such assemblies be *without music?* Music gives vivacity to all generally. It banishes for a season the dark clouds of life. Therefore if you can sing or play, do so when you are requested. Choose pieces that are sweet, lively, and animating.

Sports are in vogue

Among young people, and particularly in the country, a variety of sports, or plays, are in vogue. Some of them are fitting only for children; but others are more intellectual, and may be made sources of improvement and amusement.

Entering into the spirit of these sports, we throw off some of the restraints of a more formal intercourse. You must not forget your politeness in your hilarity, or allow yourself to 'take liberties,' or lose your sense of delicacy and propriety.

The selections of the games or sports belongs to the ladies.

Kissing

Kissing sometimes forms a part of the performances in some of these games. No true gentleman will abuse the freedom which the laws of the game allow; but if required will delicately kiss the hand of the lady. A lady will offer her lips to be kissed only to her husband and not to him in company.

Give your hand to a gentleman to kiss, your cheek to a friend, but keep your lips for your lover.

THE BALL ROOM

Nothing is more preposterous than to eat in gloves

Music is absolutely necessary, as piano, violin, flute, &c. It is always best to engage the attendance of a professional pianist.

According to fashion in towns ten o'clock is early enough to present yourself at a dance. In the country, you should go earlier.

Draw on your gloves in the dressing-room, and do not remove them in the dancing rooms. At supper take them off; nothing is more preposterous than to eat in gloves.

Supper, if one be provided, takes place about midnight, and is not closed till the end of the ball. A lady should not drink much wine, and never more than one glass of champagne.

A lady's guide to dancing

If a gentleman offers to dance with a lady, she should *not* refuse, unless for some *valid* reason.

When an unpractised dancer makes a mistake, it would be very impolite to have the air of giving her a lesson.

Unless a lady has a very graceful figure, and can use it with great elegance, it is better for her to *walk* through the quadrilles.

At the end of the dance, the gentleman reconducts the lady to her place, bows and thanks her. She also bows in silence.

Ladies who dance much should be careful not to boast before those who dance but little.

To avoid the scramble, purchase tickets, &c., in advance
and be in good time.

TRAVELLING

Life is a journey, and we are all fellow-travellers

Under no circumstances is courtesy more demanded, than in travelling. In the scramble for tickets, seats, or state-rooms, good manners are frequently elbowed aside and trampled under foot.

Acknowledge the kindness

The pleasantest seats belong to the ladies. But many ladies never acknowledge the kindness of a gentleman in giving up his seat, but settle themselves down as if they were entitled to them by divine right.

Opening the window

You have no right to keep a window open if the current of air thus produced annoy another. There are a sufficient number of discomforts in travelling, and it should be the aim of each passenger to lessen them as much as possible.

A lady's guide to receiving visitors politely
When anyone enters, rise immediately, advance towards him, and request them to sit down.

If it is a young man, *offer* him an arm-chair.

If an elderly man, *insist* upon his *accepting* the arm-chair; if a lady, let her be seated upon the sofa.

If the mistress of the house is intimate with the lady who visits her, she will place herself near her.

If the visitor is a stranger, the mistress of the house rises, and any persons who may be already in the room should do the same.

RECEIVING COMPANY

An easy, quiet, and self-possessed manner

The duty of receiving visitors usually devolves upon the mistress of the house, and should be performed in an easy, quiet, and self-possessed manner. In this way you will put your guests at their ease and make their call or visit pleasant both to them and to yourself.

Make a call tolerable

Quiet self-possession and unaffected courtesy will enable you to make even a ceremonious morning call tolerable, if not absolutely pleasant to both the caller and yourself.

The corner of the fireplace

In the winter the most honourable places are those at the corners of the fireplace.

Miscellaneous Hints for Ladies

You should never ask any person at table to help you to anything; always apply to the servants.

⊷•◦•◦•⊷

Curtseying is obsolete. Ladies now universally bow instead. The latter is more convenient, if not a more graceful form of salutation.

⊷•◦•◦•⊷

Inattention to dress bespeaks a contempt for the people with whom you mingle.

⊷•◦•◦•⊷

The simpler and more easy your manners, the more you will impress people of your good breeding. *Affectation* is one of the brazen marks of vulgarity.

Miscellaneous Hints for Ladies

Affectation is the vain and foolish attempt to appear wise and rich. The lady who gives herself airs of importance only exhibits the proofs of weakness.

A present should be made with as little parade and ceremony as possible.

Nothing detracts more from the character of a real lady than the exhibition of envy.

It is a mark of ill-breeding to refuse praise where praise is evidently due; and nothing is more vulgar than indiscriminate and insincere praise.

An overdone politeness is the next thing to rudeness.

Miscellaneous Hints for Ladies

Avoid going into company when you are what is called *out of sorts,* and dull. People get together to enjoy themselves, and if you are not in a condition to *enjoy* by all means stay at home.

Do not pretend to be what you are not, for the thin veil is soon seen through, and by trying to deceive, you will be judged an impostor and, as such, excluded from society.

Of all the sinners against the laws of politeness, the *bragger* or the *liar* is one of the greatest. False pretending is one of the sure signs of ill-breeding.

Miscellaneous Hints for Ladies

The best manners spring from the best heart.
The gifts made by ladies are of the most refined
nature possible: they should be little articles not
purchased, but deriving a priceless value as being the
off-spring of their gentle skill; a little picture from
their pencil or a trifle from their needle.

LOVE AND COURTSHIP
PRELIMINARY REMARKS

֍

Without these you are never *fit to marry*

Who, at one period or another, has not loved? Even in minds which seem to derive no pleasure from anything, there must have been felt the power of love, compelling them to seek happiness by sharing life with another; to look with another's eyes; to be joyed by another's pleasures, and be pained by another's griefs.

A woman's perceptions are keener

Women reach maturity earlier than men, and many marry earlier. Her perceptions are keener and her sensibilities finer, and she may trust more to *instinct*, but she should add a knowledge of her physical and mental constitution, and of whatever relates to the requirements of sound *health*, and a *perfect development* cannot be over-rated. *Without these you are never fit to marry.*

Delicacy

If you feel anything in the conduct or language of a gentleman that gives you reason to believe that he wishes to engage your affections, act as good sense and delicacy shall dictate. In the first place, lay the matter before your parents or guardians, who you may be sure have your interests and happiness at heart.

Do not permit his attentions

If you cannot love him wholly and solely, do not allow his addresses, however gratifying; do not permit his attentions, if you cannot give him hand and heart; such coquetting is highly blamable, and has frequently marred the happiness of many a worthy man.

A lady's guide to choosing a husband
In choosing a husband, the discreet young woman
will attentively look:

~ to the conversation of men;

~ to the manner in which they spend their time;

~ how they employ the money they get;

~ if they are of low or aspiring notions;

~ if they love the company of the lewd and profane;

~ if they are self-sufficient, foppish or vain.

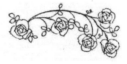

*These are indispensable things to be weighed in a contract
that may last for life.*

CAUTIONS

Do not unite with extravagance

In seeking a partner for life, look to it that you be not entrapped by beauty of person merely. Choose a man of intelligence. Seek gentleness of spirit. Seek a lover of home. Let it be one whom, to use the beautiful Arabian proverb, *"you can make the keeper of your soul"*.

Tastes and habits

Be cautious respecting the disposition, tastes, and habits of your intended. The pleasure of the one should be reflected in the mind and actions of the other.

Do not unite with extravagance. The want of economy, wastefulness, uncleanly habits, and want of management would be a source of regret and might cause bitter altercation.

A cheerful home is the best security for happiness.
A well-lighted room, nicely cooked and well-served
dinner and everything bright and clean
produce pleasant impressions.

The duties of married life

Good manners are not to be put on and off with
one's best clothes. Politeness is an article for every-
day wear. The true lady is a lady at all times.
A snob is a *snob* always and everywhere.

On the wife especially devolves the privilege and
pleasure of rendering home happy. Let not your
husband have cause to complain that you are more
agreeable abroad than at home.

Have the comfort and happiness of your husband
always in view.

Avoid all bickerings: what does it signify where a
picture hangs or whether a rose or fern looks best
on the drawing-room table?

SELF–COMMAND

Control of all your words and actions

Without perfect self-control you are constantly liable to do something amiss. You must not only be conscious who you are, where you are, and what you are about, but you must also have a complete control of all your words and actions and feel *at home* wherever you are.

Bashfulness or excitement
You are liable to lose this self–command either through bashfulness or excitement. The former can be overcome by resolute effort and the cultivation of self–respect and self-reliance. Do not allow it to keep you out of society.

One of the best means of improvement in manners is observation. In company, where you are in doubt in reference to any rule or form, be quiet and observe what others do, and govern your conduct by theirs.

CHOICE OF FRIENDS

Distrust and friendship never dwell together

Be slow and cautious in contracting a friendship. Endeavour to find a friend whose goodness of heart and intelligence will render such a connection honourable and beneficial.

Have no secrets

Having formed a friendship, and proved your friend worthy of the name, have no secrets from her. Distrust and friendship never dwell together; a generous, confiding disposition is at all times happier than a reserved and suspicious one.

Hold sacred the secrets of others

However candid and explicit you may think proper to be on your own affairs, *remember to hold sacred the secrets of others, they belong not to you, therefore you have no right to make use of them.*

Certain unguarded moments

If you are a single woman, never make a friend and confidante of a married one, for however honourable and trustworthy you may consider her, there are certain unguarded moments, when a woman says things to her husband, that at other times she would blush to find herself guilty of.

Woman's natural temper and disposition cause her to form friendships more eagerly.

Never make friends of your servants

Never stoop to the degradation of making confidantes of your servants; the moment you do so, you place yourself on a level with them, and no longer command respect. Be kind to them and make their situation as comfortable as possible. Never treat them as equals.

BEWARE OF FLATTERERS

Smooth talk is often sweet poison

Choose persons for friends in whom you can really trust. Beware of flatterers, for smooth talk is often sweet poison. Flattery calls white, black, and black, white. Guard against it.

Qualifications

Few people have all the qualifications one would look for in a friend. The fundamental points are a virtuous disposition, a good understanding, solid judgement, sweetness of temper, steadiness of mind, and sincerity of heart.

One or two

Expect not many friends, but think yourself happy, if through life, you meet with one or two who deserve that name.

ACCENT

*Let your accent be well marked and sustained, if you desire
to speak or read with brilliancy and effect*

There are two ways of accenting words. In words of
Anglo-Saxon origin the accent is generally on the
root; as *love, love'ly*.

In words derived from the Latin and Greek, the accent
is generally on the termination, as *error*, or *erro'neous*.

In words used both as nouns and as verbs, the verb has
generally the accent on the latter and the noun on the
former syllable; as *to cement, a ce'ment*.

Unaccented vowels are often enunciated imperfectly,
or not at all. *Beware of this fault.* Each letter that is not
silent, should tell upon the ear in its true character.

HOW TO PRONOUNCE

Tones which fall so pleasantly

Many persons pronounce badly; but by attending to the following observations, they may become correct speakers.

Keep the lips free

Sit or stand erect, with the shoulders thrown back, to facilitate deep breathing; open the mouth and keep the lips free, that the sounds may flow with clearness and precision.

In this way we can emit the full, round, sonorous tones which fall so pleasantly upon the cultivated ear.

Now read and re-read the following, emphasising the italic words.

The pilgrim *fathers*, where are they?
The waves that brought them o'er,
Still roll in the bay, and throw their *spray*,
As they break along the *shore*;
Still roll in the *bay* as they rolled that *day*,
When the *May* Flower moored below;
When the *sea* around was black with *storms*,
And *white* the *shore* with *snow*.

Be careful, to avoid sharp, rough, husky, and guttural tones.
Fullness, roundness, smoothness, sweetness, and purity are
the qualities of tone after which you should strive.

A shrill, piping voice

A very low pitch of voice is sometimes impressive, but this extreme should be avoided. A very high pitch, however, is a still worse fault! Nothing is more disagreeable than a shrill, piping voice.

A lady's guide to pronouncing words

Do not hurry your enunciation of words,
precipitating syllable over syllable and word over
word; nor melt them into a mass of confusion.

Do not abridge or prolong them too much, but
deliver them from your vocal organs as golden coins
from the mint, distinctly stamped and of full weight.

Words are not to be hurried over, they should not
be trailed, or drawled, nor permitted to slip out
carelessly, so as to drop unfinished.

Very loud speaking is vulgar and unnecessary. Speak
deliberately and distinctly and you will be heard
and understood.

A lady's guide to pronouncing words

It is better to be *natural* than *mechanically correct*.

The letter *r* is often imperfectly sounded. It has
properly a gentle rolling sound, and *should*
always be heard.

Some *H*englishmen *h*often misplace their haitches.
"Do you drink *h*ale in your country?" an English
cockney asked of an American. "No," the latter
replied; "we drink thunder and lightning!"

Be particularly careful to place the accent on the
right syllable; as, al-*lies*, in-*qui*-ry.

Be careful to sound the d at the end of words.
Never say you'n I, pen un ink.

Errors of Common Talk

The English is undoubtedly the noblest of
modern tongues; but no other language of a
civilised people is so badly spoken and written.
Our mother tongue – the strong, copious,
flexible Anglo-Saxon – is *our richest inheritance*.
It is not so difficult a task to master it thoroughly
as is generally supposed.
By reading the errors of common talk you may
impress on your memory the correct accent and
form of expression and thus avoid the false.

FALSE PRONUNCIATION

If you get nothing else …

Mis–chievous has the accent on the first syllable. The following words are often wrongly accented. Place the accent on the italic syllables:

Ac-*cept*-able   *Moun*tainous

*Con*trary   *For*midable

Geo*met*rical

Again should be pronounced a-gen

Apostle, let the t be silent

Drought, properly pronounced, should rhyme with *sprout*

Be careful not to omit the first *r* in partridge

Desire, should have the sound of z

If you get nothing else, get an education!

THE ASPIRATE

Some persons aspirate where the h should be silent

Many persons *omit* the *aspirate* at the beginning of words, and also after the w, as in where; and in the middle of words, as in forehead which they mispronounce for-*ed* instead of for*h*ed.

The silent h

Some persons aspirate where there is no h, or where it should be silent, as *hample* for ample. Before a *silent h*, the article *an* is used, and not *a*; as, an herbalist.

Feel the breath

Loudness of voice is not aspiration. Hold up the hand a little before your mouth, and pronounce a word beginning with *h*, and which you *should* aspirate. If you aspirate, you will feel the breath against your hand; but if you do not feel it, you *only speak louder*.

USING THE WRONG WORD

Very common errors …

"I expect the books were sent yesterday." This is wrong, because we expect that only which is yet in the future. You may expect that the books will be sent tomorrow, or next week, or next year; but you *think, conclude,* or *suspect* that they were sent yesterday.

"Mr. Rapley *learned* me grammar." He may have *taught* you. The teacher *teaches*; and the pupil *learns*.

"Seldom *or ever* see her." Say seldom *or never,* or seldom *if ever*.

To use an adjective in place of an adverb; as "This letter is written *shocking*," is a very common error, but the opposite fault of substituting an adverb for an adjective as, "Louisa looked *beautifully*" (beautiful) is still more common. We employ adverbs to qualify verbs, it is true; but when we say "Louisa looks *beautiful*" the word beautiful, by the help of the verb looks, describes Louisa. Louisa does not perform the act of looking. We look at her.

You do not differ *with* another person but *from* him.

"I will think *on* thee, love" Say *of* thee.
Free *of* blame. Say free *from* blame.

In the winter it is said to be "dangerous to walk *of* a rainy morning." *On* a rainy morning.

Superfluous words

"The fruit was gathered off *of* that tree"

"Her conduct was approved *of*"

"Please give me both *of* those books"

Ellen rose *up* and left the room

"Who has *got* my inkstand?"

FALSE INFLECTION AND CONSTRUCTION

❦

The proper word

Please bring me *them* books. Say *those* books

Him and *me* are going to the theatre. *He* and *I* are going, is the correct expression.

She said to the shop-keeper, "If this cloth *be* good, I will purchase twenty yards of it." She should have said, "If this cloth *is* good, &c."

Shall and will

Shall and *will* are both used to express future time, and their proper application constitutes one of the difficulties of the language. When the future is to be expressed simply without emphasis, *shall* must be used after the first person and *will* after the second and third but when the future is to be expressed with determination, *will* should be used after the first person and *shall* after the second and third. If we wish to express will or determination with regard to the future, we must use *will* and not shall. If, on the other hand, we merely foretell a future event, *shall* must be used."

Should and would are both subject
to the same rules as shall and will.

"He got *on to* the stage-coach at Leedsville."
Why use two prepositions when one would be quite as explicit and far more elegant?

"*To who* was the order given?" Should be to *whom*.

"The money was divided *between* fifty." Say, *among* fifty.

"The dinner was *ate* in silence." Say *eaten*.

VULGARISMS AND SLANG

Such words should be avoided

Carefully avoid using vulgar and unmeaning words and phrases and slang. A few of the current vulgarisms of the day are:

Young ones, for *children*
Winder, for *window*
Piller, for *pillow*
Haint, for *has not*
Gal, for *girl*
Fetch, for *bring*

Such words as helter-skelter, hurly-burly, topsy-turvy,
though sometimes allowable, should generally be avoided.

The apples *what* you gave me. Say *which*.
How's yourself to-day? Is a vulgar form of salutation.
How are you? Is much better.

A dull repetition of words or sounds on nearly the same pitch is very disagreeable to the ear, and disgusting to correct taste. To avoid this fault you must first get, by practice, the full control of your vocal organs and then, entering perfectly into the spirit of what you read, allow thought and feeling to have their natural expression.

HOW TO TALK

A few faults to be avoided

Avoid rapidity and indistinctness of utterance; also a drawling, mincing, harsh, mouthing, artificial, rumbling, monotonous, whining, stately, pompous, unvaried, wavering, sleepy, boisterous, laboured, formal, faltering, trembling, heavy, theatrical, affected, and self-complacent manner; and read, speak, sing in such a clear, strong, melodious, flexible, winning, bold, sonorous, forcible, round, full, open, brilliant, natural, agreeable, or mellow tone, as the sentiment required; which contains in itself so sweet a charm, that it almost atones for the absence of argument, sense, and fancy.

A MAXIM TO BE REMEMBERED

Natural

Read just as you would naturally speak on the same subject and under similar circumstances; so that if any one should hear you without seeing you, he could not tell whether you were reading or speaking.

COMPOSITION

Habit of neatness and exactness

Composition consists in putting together in a natural order thoughts belonging to a subject. 'Description' is the first principle of composition. Description is a putting together of our impressions of any subject or scene. Practise, by copying short pieces in prose from some good writers. This will give the habit of neatness and exactness.

RULES FOR CORRESPONDENCE

1. Before you commence writing a letter, acquire a clear and distinct conception of those things on which you are about to write.

2. Strictly adhere to the rules of grammar, and express the same sentiments that you would if conversing with the person to whom you are writing.

3. Begin the letter on the top, at the right hand; write the name of the place in which you live, the day of the month, and the year.

4. Then a little below, at the left hand, write Sir, or Madam, if the person whom you are addressing is a stranger; but Dear Sir, or Dear Madam, if a friend.

5. Reserve a space for the seal, that no part of the letter may be torn when the letter is opened. Fold, direct, and seal the letter neatly.

RULES FOR PUNCTUATION

In speaking or reading a sentence, various pauses are made for the purpose of making the construction, meaning, and delivery, more distinct.

The comma

1. The simple clauses of a compound sentence are separated by a comma *"Good ladies are esteemed, and they are happy."*

2, When two or more words – whether nouns, adjectives, pronouns, verbs, or adverbs – are connected without the conjunction being expressed, the comma supplies the place of that word: *"My parents, brothers, and sisters were all present."*

3. Absolute, relative, and generally, all parenthetical and explanatory clauses, are separated from the other parts of a sentence by commas.

4. The modifying words or phrases, *nay*, *however*, *hence*, *in short*, *at least*, and *the like*, are separated by commas.

5. The words of another writer cited, but not formally introduced as a quotation, are separated by a comma.

6. A comma is used between the two parts of a sentence that has its natural order inverted.

The Semicolon

1. A sentence consisting of two parts, the one containing a complete proposition, and the other added as an inference. The two parts are separated by a semicolon.

2. A sentence consisting of several clauses, each constituting a distinct proposition, and having a dependence upon each other, are separated by semicolons.

The colon

The colon marks a longer pause than the semicolon, and is used when the sense is complete, but when there is something still behind, which tends to make the sense fuller or clearer.

1. A colon generally precedes a quotation.

2. When a sentence which consists of an enumeration of particulars, each separated from the other by a semicolon, has its sense suspended till the last clause, that clause is disjoined from the preceding by a colon.

Dash

The dash marks a break in the sentence, or an abrupt turn.

The full point

1. The full point is used at the end of every complete sentence.

2. Besides being used to mark the completion of a sentence, the full point is placed after initials.

Parenthesis

A parenthesis is used to enclose a phrase to assist in elucidating the subject, or to add force to the assertions. It ought to be sparingly used.

Apostrophe

A mark of elision, indicates that a letter is left out; as lov'd for loved, don't for do not. It is used to denote the possessive case of nouns: My girl's book.

Hyphen

A hyphen is used to connect words or part of words: as in tea-pot.

WHAT BOOKS TO READ

Read such books as will enrich the mind, improve the heart, and add to the happiness and usefulness of your life

What shall we read?

This question is often asked by those whose vocations preclude study and reading during the day, and who desire to make useful books their companions during a portion, at least, of the long evenings.

Household words

There are certain works, the contents of which have become 'household words'. Who has not read *Aesop's Fables*, *Robinson Crusoe* and *The Vicar of Wakefield* are almost universally known.   They should be read, as every well-informed person must know something about them. Shakespeare's plays and Milton's *Paradise Lost* should be added to the list.

Read as many good books as you can
whether you find them on lists or not.
Read always for the improvement of mind and heart.

How to acquire a taste for reading

And now a few words for persons who are not fond of books, but who would give much for a taste which they acknowledge to be the source of great pleasure.

Make this your starting-point

If there is a particular subject in which you are more than ordinarily interested, make this your starting-point.

A mistake

The mistake generally made by those who desire to beget in the young a taste for reading, lies in trying to force prematurely an appetite for *serious* words.

Exercises for reading

Practise. Practise. Practise. Nothing will contribute more to your success in the cultivation and management of the voice, and to deliver in a perfectly free and natural manner, short passages from poems and other literary compositions.

The Basis of Human Happiness

The basis of human happiness is truth; without this virtue, there is no reliance upon language; no confidence in friendship and no security in promises and oaths.

Truth is always consistent with itself, and needs nothing to help it out: it is always near at hand, and sits upon our lips, and is ready to drop out before we are aware. Whereas a lie is troublesome, and sets a lady's invention on the rack, and one trick needs a good many more of the same kind to make it good.

Other Copper Beech Gift Books to collect:-

HOW TO ENTERTAIN YOUR GUESTS
A 1911 collection of indoor games
A companion book to 'The Duties of Servants'

THE DUTIES OF SERVANTS
The routine of domestic service in 1890.
Reproduced for your enjoyment now.

THE LADY'S DRESSING ROOM
Open the door to beauty and relaxation secrets from
days gone by. How to get up, fresh, beautiful and in an
amiable frame of mind with all your wrinkles smoothed
over - and other
fragrant tips from a golden age!

SOCIAL SUCCESS
The modern girl's guide to confidence, poise,
manners and tact.
1930s etiquette for all occasions.

THE SERVANTLESS HOUSEHOLD
How to cope - some polite advice

APPEARANCES
How to keep them up on a limited income

DAINTY DISHES
for slender incomes

KITCHEN COSMETICS
Beauty from the pantry

HALVING THE HOUSEWORK
Valuable 'retro' style advice from the 1950s

For your free catalogue containing these and other titles write to:

Copper Beech Publishing Ltd
P O Box 159 East Grinstead
Sussex England RH19 4FS
www.copperbeechpublishing.co.uk

www.copperbeechpublishing.co.uk